ASTRO JOURNAL

THE ASTROLOGERS' JOURNAL FOR RECORDING TRANSITS

PREPARED BY

RIKKI BLYTHE

FISHTAIL ARTS & ASTROLOGY

EPIGRAPH

A journal for astrologers.

We are like comets, tearing through the universe, leaving a trail of memories, our future stability uncertain. All we have is this moment, a comet ablaze, tearing through the universe.

Cycles within cycles, never one moment the same, the mystery thickens and we can forget.

The mass trivialization of existence makes it very difficult to interest more people into mystical realms of thought. Astrologers have maintained their independence for thousands of years.

To those who know the value of astrology may you grow from inside out, blissfully happy.

Illustration *1

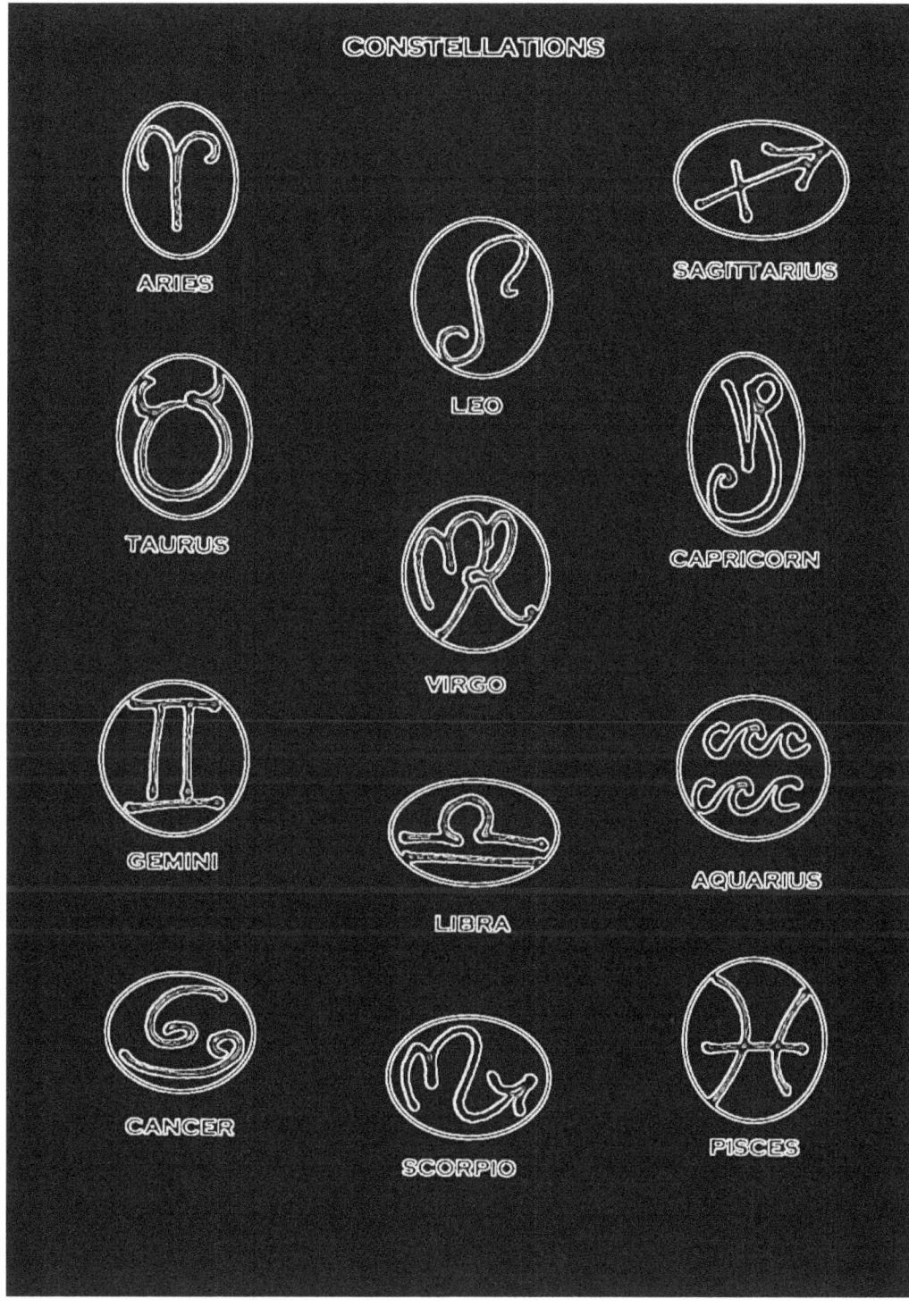

Illustration *2

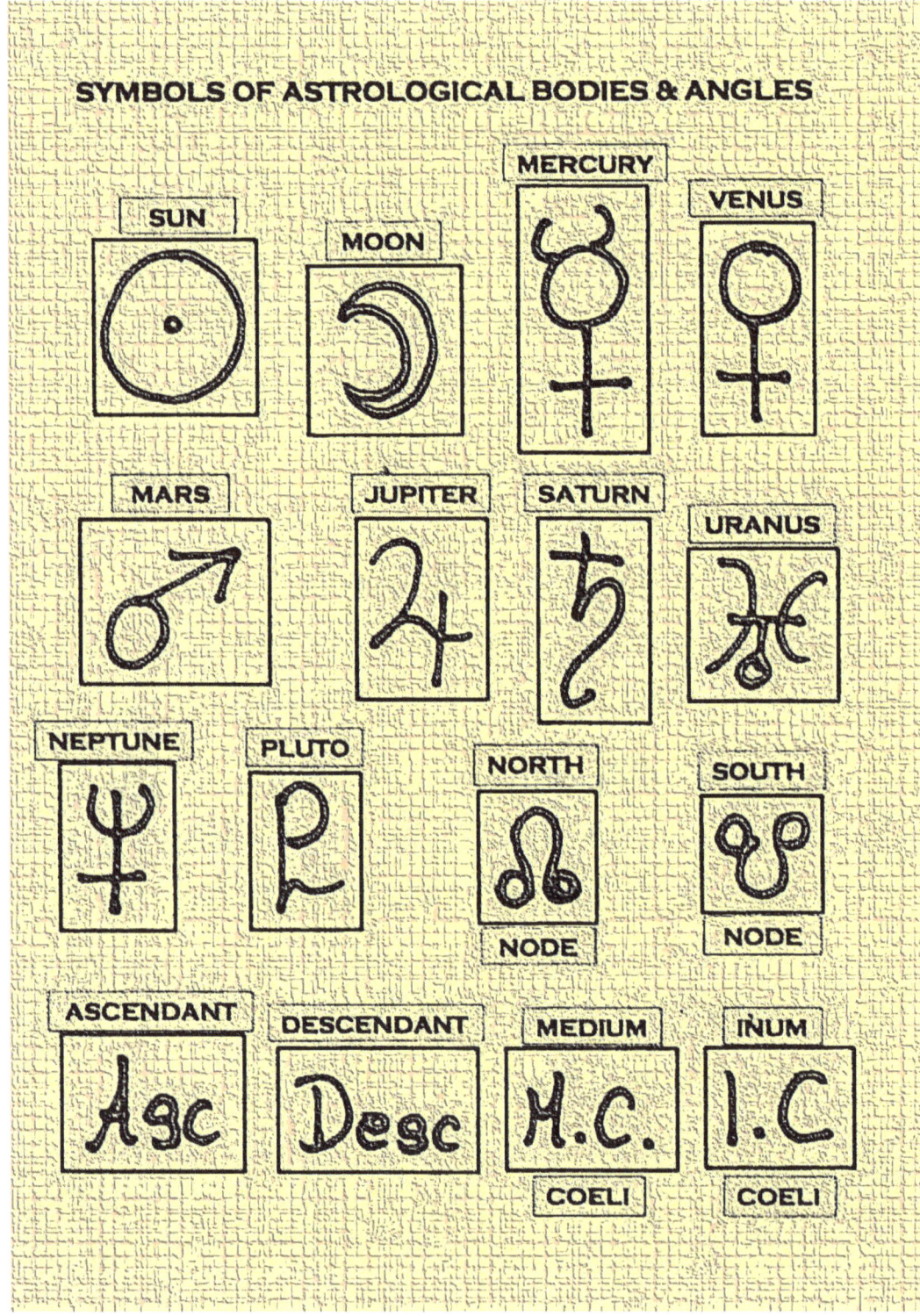

Illustration *3
SYMBOLS OF THE ASPECTS

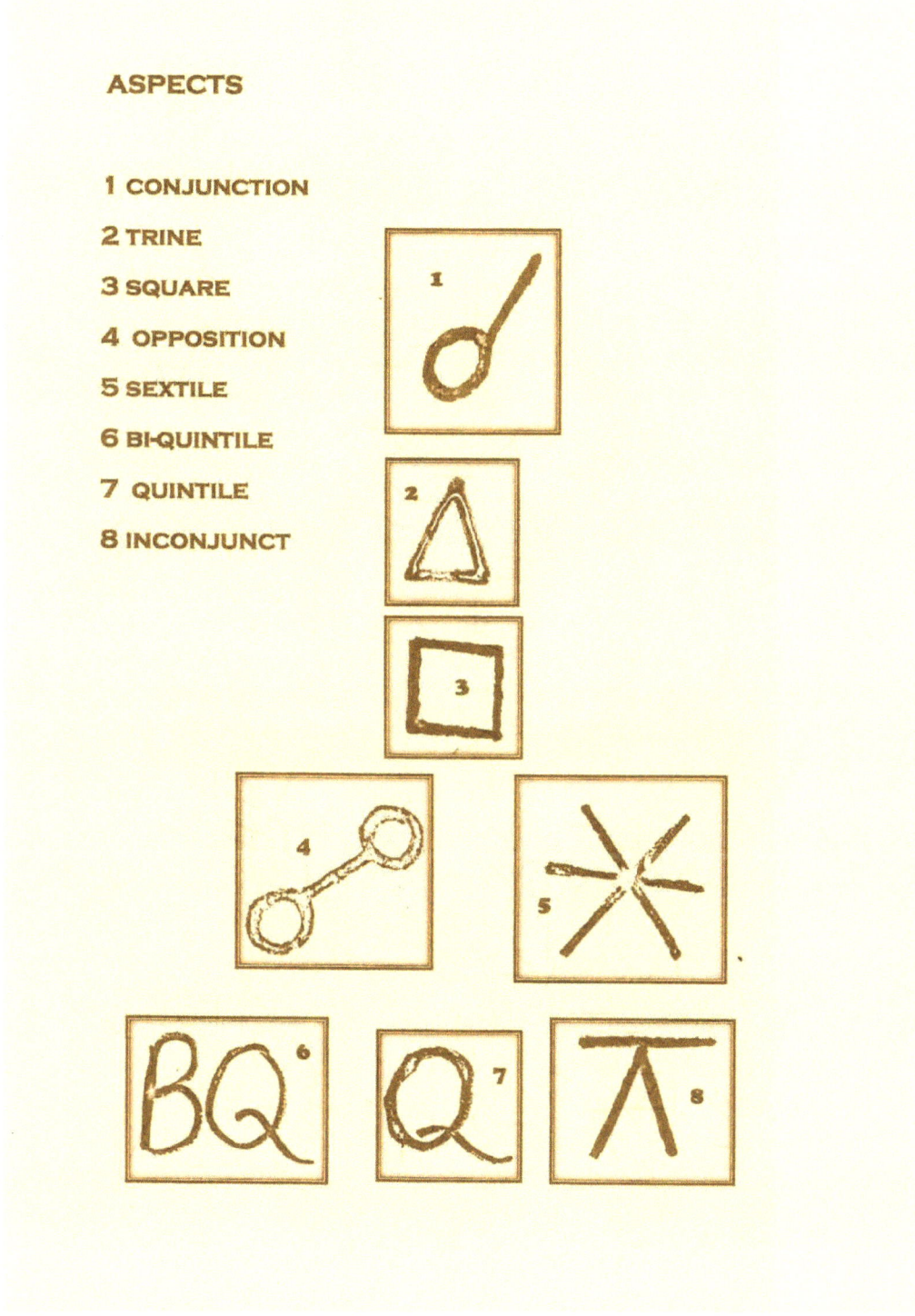

Illustration *4

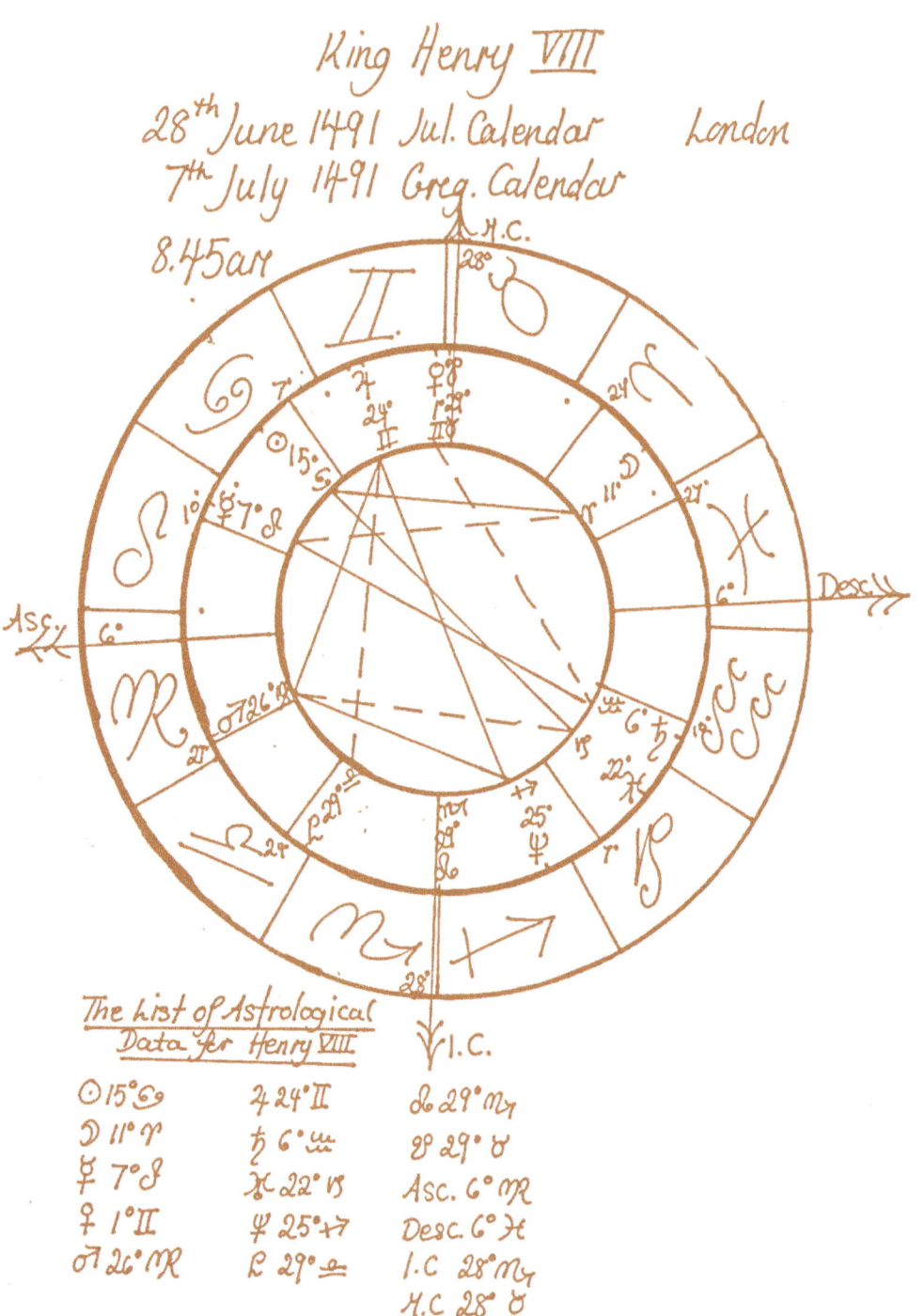

MOON Transits

MOON TRANSITS

The Moon transits the whole horoscope once a lunar month so perhaps the feelings you will come across will be easily recognized, as they will have happened many times.

The Moon brings a feeling like a need or an emotion. It is not necessarily loud but it can spur you to a small action which may seem like nothing much; such as ringing your mother, choosing to work or staying in or greeting people like you are on top of the world. You will notice that nearly always the same transit inspires the same thing.

Our emotional nature is entwined with our well-being and so little things like tidying our house or doing a weekly shop can make us feel stable, comforted and well. We start noticing life-style patterns. These are small patterns, the parts of life that are often taken for granted. If we always shop on Wednesdays but one Wednesday the Moon conjuncts Uranus, we might want to do something more exciting. Or if it conjuncts Mars, we might have a spat with another customer. But if it conjuncts Jupiter there might be nothing else we want to do except a big shop for food.

The above examples are grossly over-simplified; because if our Natal Moon is conjunct Uranus and square Mercury, we probably don't do food shopping regularly and, instead, prefer to eat take-away and quickly prepared food. The natal placement of our Moon, with its aspects, constellation and House will provide the field of action, and only over time will you learn which area is the main domain of your Moon. But within that field are the inner workings of Moon nature.

Generally though, the Moon rules inspirations, decisions and choices around food, home, comfort, family, body and habits, and affects our mood and health. Take notice of what you need.

Transiting Moon - Natal Sun

OK to be me

The way I often am

Comfortable expressing how I am

Transiting Moon - Natal Moon

Cycles. Cycles of people, of feelings

Keep coming back here

The comfort I need

Transiting Moon - Natal Mercury

Siblings, cousins, close friends

Familial communication

Need to talk deeply, personally

Transiting Moon - Natal Venus

I would like more meaning

Can I love more?

Can things be more beautiful?

Lonely/solitude or socializing?

Transiting Moon - Natal Mars

Spice things up a bit

Is that enough?

My sexy, powerful body

What do I need to do?

Transiting Moon - Natal Jupiter

Generous helpings

For me and everyone

Fitting it all in

Transiting Moon - Natal Saturn

I would rather be alone right now

Working

Fixing and maintaining

Staying small

Transiting Moon - Natal Uranus

Of course I could create chaos

And if I must, I could stick to routine

I could add something new

But I cannot just sit here

Transiting Moon - Natal Neptune

Captured by music

Routines sway

Sea of emotions

Gentleness, a gift

Transiting Moon - Natal Pluto

I feel what I need with a determination

I will hold on to this determination

Don't mess with me

I exist and I need

Transiting Moon - Natal North Node

Tricky this

Not sure I am quite right

But it feels sort of special

Could be important

Transiting Moon - Natal South Node

Ahh yes I am rather comfortable

Used to this

Quite talented really

Transiting Moon - Ascendant

I feel people can see me

What shall I let them see?

Familiar environment

Transiting Moon - Descendant

My chosen few

I grace you with my favouritism

And lavish the attention I need from you...

...back

Transiting Moon - M.C

They see I am right

Deserving

In tune with what is required

Transiting Moon - I.C

Stay home

Cook, tidy, prepare

Keep me and others in my nest

SUN transits

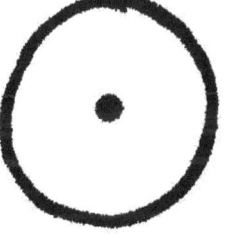

SUN TRANSITS

The Sun transits and prods our integrity by highlighting parts of our life. We experience the full benefit of joy from the Sun when we find a way to integrate our spontaneous nature with the moment. The moment can bring anything; the moment cannot be prepared for except through confidence and self-belief. The Sun represents confidence, self-belief, spontaneity and integrity. When the time comes we will stand up, be ourselves, and respond fully.

The inner strength and childishness of the Sun nature is ever-flowering as new character expressions and new ways of being are integrated. Everything offers the Sun opportunity to grow. Age, death, a walk in the park, huge projects – everything. The Sun is like the eternal child forever discovering a new way of being, expressing untried and untested behaviours in response to the ever-changing moment.

But if our Sun is afflicted with a sense of lacking or tremulousness it might be difficult to experience the joy. At least through watching transits you can see what you are pushing away, then over time, bring in self-belief and trust.

Sun signs have a lot of power and influence in our lives as it is the part of us which is inspiring, individual and a guiding light. But if people follow us they lose themselves, just as we lose ourselves if we blindly copy others. Individually we have to find trust in ourselves. Individually we grow the way we grow in response to our own ever changing moment.

Take notice of being present.

Transiting Sun – Natal Sun

Happy Birthday!

Spontaneity – check

Because you deserve it

Transiting Sun - Natal Moon

Wake-up!

This is a brand new day

Let's do it again

The way I like things

Transiting Sun - Natal Mercury

Speak truth

Blind them with words

Is this journey worth it?

Transiting Sun - Natal Venus

Mirror mirror

I see your flaws

Your beauty too

Value and play

Transiting Sun - Natal Mars

Let's do it!

Whoa! So right!

Yes! Dare

Transiting Sun - Natal Jupiter

Encouraging, there is abundance

I am in it

Lush, lucky

Transiting Sun - Natal Saturn

Great wise being

Room for manoeuvre within traditions

Lighten up a bit

Transiting Sun - Natal Uranus

Hello friend, alien, animal

What is new?

Fantastic idea

Wired today

Transiting Sun - Natal Neptune

Religion of our fathers

Kind men

Space to experience divine

Flowing

Escape

Transiting Sun - Natal Pluto

Things need changing

Renovating

Conforming to my will

Transiting Sun - Natal North Node

Other people can and do

Make space for future

Here

Now

Transiting Sun - Natal South Node

Must've been reincarnated

I am that good here

Even if it's bad

I effectively do it

Transiting Sun - Ascendant

Shine on me moving

In action, animating

This body, this way

Transiting Sun - Descendant

So glad you are here

You are vibrant

Good to be with

Transiting Sun - M.C

The way to heaven is through me

I am pointing up

A conduit for ambition

Transiting Sun - I.C

Home is where my heart is

The threshold shines

Retreat

Hold court

MERCURY
transits

☿

MERCURY TRANSITS

When Mercury transits, in the horoscope, inner energy is triggered to communicate. Mercury moves through words, via wind, or bodily transported via car or tube or bus or web.

The principle of Mercury is to transport concepts and ideas. Whether that idea is in a person or in their mind, Mercury moves itself nearer its reception. Communication through a slight warm touch of a hand, a wicked stare, an out flow of words, and an advertising pitch are all moving flashes of thought.

What is the message? Mercury's realm is the message. The meaning in the symbol; the thoughts conveyed by warm hands or glaring eyes, the presence of a body strong and supportive are some of the myriad of ways a message can be given.

Transits by Mercury are opportunities to give or receive or share meanings. They can be apparently trite, such as 'eating aubergines is a good thing', only to later discover it opened the conversation with someone else.

How you communicate is shown by the House, constellation and aspects of Natal Mercury. Transiting Mercury comes unencumbered by any of your learned inhibitions or ways but you might find yourself choosing to use the same track of mind you have already learned. Also, the Planets' House, constellation and aspect that is being transited by Mercury, may be open or closed to the Messenger. Take notice of what you are thinking.

Transiting Mercury - Natal Sun

Messages

Reveal what is hidden

Shine on a bigger picture

Transiting Mercury - Natal Moon

Needing to communicate

Feeling the sense of connection

Belonging

Reaching out

Transiting Mercury - Natal Mercury

Letters and emails

Telephone calls and conversations

Conveying thoughts and small journeys

Transiting Mercury - Natal Venus

Network, socialize

Chatting away smiling

Pleasantly expressive in company

Transiting Mercury - Natal Mars

Either someone narks you with their words

Or you nark them

And so on

Or, you start

So you say what you want carefully

Transiting Mercury - Natal Jupiter

Flexible thinking

Big ideas, meaningful connections

Travelling

Earth, land, roads

Transiting Mercury - Natal Saturn

Focus

Check accounts, paperwork

Authority, old people

Small print

Transiting Mercury - Natal Uranus

Possibly very exciting

Probably probable

Interest, invent

In...

Transiting Mercury - Natal Neptune

Listening to music

Words that sway

Sounds which awaken fascination

Stories and dreams

Transiting Mercury - Natal Pluto

Words to make change

Insight

Psychological

Hidden truths

Transiting Mercury - Natal North Node

Read new articles

Honour future maybe's

Adverts for new skills

Transiting Mercury - Natal South Node

Always talking this way

Thinking this way

Good at it

Wanting more; but what?

Transiting Mercury - Ascendant

I am saying what I am about

Where I am going

Today, tomorrow, next year

What image do I give?

Transiting Mercury - Descendant

Get a word in edgeways

Straight to their ears

Make that call, send that message

Transiting Mercury - M.C

How did you hear about me?

Yes I can do that

This is how it can be done

Let all the relevant people know

Transiting Mercury - I.C

House meeting

Message to do something different

Familial ways of interaction

Family visiting

Thoughts over the threshold

VENUS transits

♀

VENUS TRANSITS

Just about all of the Venus transits are enjoyable. If they are not, it is because you are blocking pleasurable feelings coming into your life.

Venus transits specifically bring a pleasant sense of well-being and value to your integrated sense of self. This is because feeling good about ourselves is an integral part of being human. We are driven to find happiness. We are driven to treasure values. Yet Venus does not drive. Venus attracts. So the realm of Venus is about attraction and giving. Magnetism. The currency in the realm of Venus is value. What do you value? Then that is what you attract.

Overall, the transits of Venus instil a sense of well-being, okayness, because our world feels good. We all have different values. These values are generally love, money and beauty. But also, a love of knowledge, of passion, of trains or rabbits. What we value attracts more of what we value.

In terms of money, not everyone really values money; they value holidays, or shoes or dining out. Maybe football, or reading. Perhaps deep conversations. So what fills that person's life? Exactly.

So don't force yourself to focus on love, money or beauty only. They are atypical values. Venus transits help you to uncover the things that really are valuable for you.

Venus awakens you to the value in each Planet it transits. Take notice of what you enjoy. Also enjoy being as attractive as you can be; it is a very natural part of us to be our most attractive; fluff your feathers!

Transiting Venus - Natal Sun

Typically Sun sign

A sure sign that the Sun sign is important

Dare to trust

Bright attraction

Transiting Venus - Natal Moon

One of the finest transits

Feeling lovely

Lush

Gorgeous

Comfortable

A definite love vibration

Transiting Venus - Natal Mercury

Charm; or at least the will to be pleasant

Smooth over cracks, by accepting them

Music and art with a message

Transiting Venus - Natal Venus

The day to gage the state of your love realm

Giving and receiving

Balanced? Unsatisfying? Obvious really

Transiting Venus - Natal Mars

Adorn, desire to compete

Sexual guiles

Creativity

Nice way of doing it

Transiting Venus - Natal Jupiter

Too lush to do much

Pleasure round every corner

Extravagance and ease

Philosophically giving in to desire

A pleasant journey

Transiting Venus - Natal Saturn

Beautifing the ritual

Long lasting relationships

Financial investments

Aging gracefully

Transiting Venus - Natal Uranus

Unique beauty, that little touch

Loving pets

Good friends and outrageous style

Transiting Venus - Natal Neptune

Meditation and transcendental experience

Never getting there

A beauty so profound it aches

Danger of collapsing in escape

Transiting Venus - Natal Pluto

Power and love, more powerful with love

Transforming power of everything sweet

Manipulative

Cunning sense of well being

Transmute cunning to compassion, if you can

Transiting Venus - Natal North Node

Ease into a new experience

Make the awkwardness beautiful

Ambience

Transiting Venus - Natal South Node

Natural beauty

A relief to let the guard down

Reap the same patch

Easy behaviour

Transiting Venus - Natal Ascendant

A new style

More expressive of self

A must have – like it belongs with me

Creating or finding those little flairs

Transiting Venus - Natal Descendant

In an ideal world your lover walks in and gives affection

Chances are you give it

Caring for important others

Transiting Venus - Natal M.C

A good day to get married

My corner of the world values what I value

Artists' exhibition preview

Beautifying something at work

Transiting Venus - Natal I.C

Grace all those who cross my threshold

With fair attention

Value what is little

Order, nest

Begin a new cycle to being a more loving being

MARS transits

MARS TRANSITS

When Mars transits, expect to be moved, motivated and inspired to take action. Holding back at this time brings depression in its wake. Though obviously, the kind of action you take should be considered. Mars is not necessarily a spontaneous lash out in anger. Mars definitely rules anger; but how you deal with the energy of the anger is your responsibility.

Anger is a sign that your boundary has been overstepped. Instead of war, just strengthen your boundary! Fighting is not justified. Finding a way to keep what is yours and maintaining your boundary is important work. Anger belongs to Mars but Mars is the henchman of the Sun. Your Sun rules. Your Sun shines with true confidence. How you integrate anger and still get your way is your work. Mars has many tactics, dependant on constellation.

The speciality of Mars is a meaningful goal. Mars gives us our mojo and motivation through wanting to do something. You only want to do what matters to you. If your will is repeatedly knocked you will have a showdown with your soul as your personality crumbles; do you really want that? It may be that your will had saturated other people's desires and a transit shows you that you are a bit of a bully. Mars is passion and energy. Do not be lazy in acting for your true desires. The despair, depression and disappointment of an unlived Mars is far, far worse than the fall from failure.

As Mars transits your horoscope you get to look at what matters to you and how you are going about getting it. You get an influx of energy to do something more.

Often Mars brings anger, but it also brings the passion and desire to complete something for yourself. Take notice of what you want.

Transiting Mars - Natal Sun

Not much can stop you today

Motivated

Self-belief strengthened

Effort energized

Transiting Mars - Natal Moon

Passionate desires

Sexy oomph

Rashes and fevers

Physical needs

Transiting Mars - Natal Mercury

Argumentative, debating

Just saying, must say

Rushing journey

Speed, brilliance and danger

Transiting Mars - Natal Venus

Acting upon attraction

Effort to make money

Creative pursuits

Defending, upholding values

Transiting Mars - Natal Mars

This day or two is the seed day for the beginning of a new project, or new turn in existing project. It is the main precursor of depression if you do not take steps to uphold your magnificent life potential and take necessary action to do what you want without harming anyone.

Transiting Mars - Natal Jupiter

Strength and prowess

Energy to execute big ideas

Motivated to explore, journey, travel

Seek philosophical answers

Transiting Mars - Natal Saturn

Kick start, keep going

Add a switch, metal-work

Motivate old bones

Try to push beyond limitations, carefully

Triumph

Transiting Mars - Natal Uranus

Dare to pursue your idea

Quick off the start

Defending individuality

Flourish

Transiting Mars - Natal Neptune

Motivated to meditate

Dance like a dervish

Desire to appease, do a good turn

Transiting Mars - Natal Pluto

Bold move to prove

Reaction to or against power

Trip wire trigger for boundaries

Rage

Transiting Mars - Natal Ascendant

Red in the face; anger, embarrassment

Be true to who you are

Winner, fighter, energy

Transiting Mars - Natal Descendant

Arguments

Sexy, fiery other

Overstepped boundaries

Defending boundary

Transiting Mars - Natal North Node

The sign and house of North Node is strengthened

Respond anew

Uphold behaviours which have good consequences

Defend your right to try, despite lack of support

Transiting Mars - Natal South Node

Typical anger

Stroppy, salty, terse

Determined to do what you want

Taking without asking

Transiting Mars - M.C

Jumping up to be counted

Job interviews and career moves

Sport, challenges, games, fights

Righteousness

Transiting Mars - I.C

Ending something to begin something

Practice small, at home, unseen

Arguments and tussles behind doors

Accentuating thresholds

JUPITER transits ♃

JUPITER TRANSITS

Jupiter transits, as well as Venus transits, mark some of the loveliest and most pleasant days.

Jupiter brings hope, enthusiasm and joy. Jupiter also governs the realm of the higher mind and bestows a hunger for experience and a thirst for knowledge. Jupiter brings an optimistic world-view governed by reason.

The sense of freedom associated with Jupiter comes from a reasonable insight of accepting or fleeing limitations. The associations of travel come from exploring the world around, wanting to experience, associate and interact with more of the world.

Jupiter bigs things up. The only negative association of Jupiter is with cancer; it seems to correlate with tumours growing. Also, not making a commitment because of not wanting to lose freedom could be another negative; as could the braggadocio characteristic. However, the sense of being emotionally buoyant is often impeded through up-bringing, and so it is more likely you will not allow yourself to go too far or act out the more negative expressions of Jupiter. Being interested in life is a state of mind that is, as astrology shows, a natural state of mind. Jupiter is a wonderful teacher, who praises and encourages us to be our best.

When a transit of Jupiter occurs, it is an opportunity to experience this lighter state of mind. Transits of Jupiter are also known to be lucky.

Take notice of your good-nature.

Transiting Jupiter - Natal Sun

The year this transit occurs sends ripples of excitement through our being, as the waves of Jupiter's optimism realign our mind and spirit.

And life is very good.

Transiting Jupiter - Natal Moon

Ohh the eating which occurs at this time!

Gorgeous friends, opportunities

Comfort, everything we need

Transiting Jupiter - Natal Mercury

Writing is starred

So much to say

Travel, exploration

Listening, languages

Transiting Jupiter - Natal Venus

Abundance of love, money, pleasure

Beautiful surroundings

Relaxed and lucky

Transiting Jupiter - Natal Mars

Good muscle tone

Hand-eye co-ordination

Loads of energy

Transiting Jupiter - Natal Jupiter

Every 12 years your lucky year (Chinese)

Everything you do is tinged with enthusiasm

More effort

Self-belief

Transiting Jupiter - Natal Saturn

Expertise and wisdom

Energy and authority

Successful enterprise

Idea to fruition

Transiting Jupiter - Natal Uranus

Encouraging originality

Standing up for ideas

Brilliant, innovative

Breaking old patterns

Freedom

Transiting Jupiter - Natal Neptune

Exquisite sense of joy

Inspired to mystical meanings

Deep mind

Abundance of water and music

Transiting Jupiter - Natal Pluto

Inner healing

Faith, recovery

Positive change

Energy to do what needs to be done

Transiting Jupiter - Natal North Node

The future is now

New experiences for a skillset

Inner truth

Transiting Jupiter - Natal South Node

Freedom from old patterns

Repeating old patterns excessively

Letting go with ease

Transiting Jupiter - Ascendant

Name change

Better identity

Coming out, starting over

Happy to be me

Eating too much

Transiting Jupiter - Descendant

Lucky to meet beneficial other

Generous, open, honest

Successful law case

Freedom from limitations imposed by others

Transiting Jupiter - M.C

A plan for success

Energy for work

Theatrical turns in front of a generous audience

Transiting Jupiter - I.C

More space at home

Room for new beginnings to be practiced

Visitors

Freedom from limitations within the family

SATURN transits

♄

SATURN TRANSITS

Where Mars urges us to action and Jupiter expands our field of opportunity, Saturn enforces limitation. Suddenly, what was once joyful becomes hard work, and it may even seem to be necessary to leave it.

Saturn sharpens our mind to a critical view, honing in on detail, noticing the rubbish others would pass as OK. Saturn is a hard task-master and a life-changer.

Sometimes Saturn brings a gloom, through thoughts or loneliness. The grief Saturn can bring is saying goodbye to something old – usually an out-grown part of us that is no longer practical. Or it could be an old part of our system that is an extravagant waste of energy, considering that more important matters now need attending to.

Yet Saturn is a best friend to those who listen; Saturn brings discipline, perseverance, realistic expectations, time management, up-holding of tradition and wise authority.

Also, the fear that is often experienced with Saturn could well turn out to be a message not to go a certain way, because other things are more important and need that energy.

Saturn speaks to us through fear, loneliness and negative thoughts. Saturn does not even complement its own great wisdom; instead, it acknowledges its own authority stoically.

These transits urge us to develop a greater responsibility towards our own life. If there is a loss of energy at this time, it could be a disease; but probably it is an unconscious ploy to stop wasting time by messing around and choose a course of action and stick with it.

Notice the acceptance of life's harsh realities.

Transiting Saturn - Natal Sun

Lifting a veil in the Natal Sun's house

Laying bare realities

Focus on maintenance

The errors of your Sun sign

Getting real, staying in the moment

Transiting Saturn - Natal Moon

Impending sense of separation

Insecurity, needs not being met

Coolness

Mother yourself, kindly

Transiting Saturn - Natal Mercury

Depressing thoughts

Obsessive minutiae

Exacting speech, focused attention

Essays and other writing projects

Transiting Saturn - Natal Venus

Exposure of falsity, loneliness

Financial tightness

Be your own best friend,

Save for a rainy day, frugality, waste not

Long lasting love

Transiting Saturn - Natal Mars

Recognition of difficulty

Effort, frustration, determination

Boundaries, marking territory

Going too slow or steady?

Transiting Saturn - Natal Jupiter

Manifest big ideas

Limit excessiveness

Stick to the trodden path

Measured expansion

Transiting Saturn - Natal Saturn

Checking position

Accepting age and limitations

Re-calculating steady course

Transiting Saturn - Natal Uranus

Materializing genius invention

Owning individuality

Responsible and original

Limiting stupid ideas

Transiting Saturn - Natal Neptune

Manifesting divine, ideal art or music

Meditation practice

Swimming lessons

Kicking the habit

Letting go of the lie

Transiting Saturn - Natal Pluto

Determined change

Unnecessary force, inner transformation

Ending of things long gone

Transiting Saturn - Natal North Node

Probably a failed attempt to bring future practice into flow

Failure part of the process

Getting it right

Trying an inspired new way

Transiting Saturn - South Node

Unacknowledged limitation

Treading same wheel

A lot of effort for natural skill

Cutting the dross away

Transiting Saturn - Ascendant

Grown-up, taking responsibility

Going it alone

Busy managing transformation

Braving the light

Transiting Saturn - Descendant

Cutting away bad habits with important people

Being real with others

Recognizing other people's limitations

Painful loss

Transiting Saturn - M.C

Deserved success or failure

Obvious efforts exposed

Craving acknowledgement

Accepted authority and experience

Transiting Saturn - I.C

Chooses limitation, acceptance of loss

Be small

Stay home

Maintain core

URANUS

transits

⛢

URANUS TRANSITS

The transits of Uranus are said to be suddenly effective when it is within a degree of the astrological body being transited. Astrologers attribute the sudden impact of Uranus to prolonged disgruntlement that has been accepted as the norm: then, when Uranus reaches its specific degree, the native acts decisively without consultations. Uranus rules the realm of originality and independence, which has the state of mind of deferring to their own judgement; no-one else needs to be consulted.

Uranus transits also bring excited, wired feelings which often wake you in the night with profound ideas. It is a good idea to keep a notebook by the bed during these transits.

You may not feel particularly daring or a creative force but other people will instinctively recognize your power to behave erratically and possibly disruptively. Even if you are projecting this nature on to someone else you are probably acting disruptively, causing people to be wary of you.

Unexpected things occur under the dominion of Uranus. In fact, your need for excitement might be so strong you seek the unusual and thrilling experiences.

Uranus represents speed and flying, also creative thinking. There is a desire to be more awake, whilst taking part in new experiences.

Brilliant ideas, technology, pets (and even aliens) bring new experiences. Fighting for the under-dog, campaigning against the status-quo and being reckless are ways of expressing daring and a treasured sense of uniqueness.

Transiting Uranus - Natal Sun

Me. Myself. I

Unusual, daring and spontaneous

Yes!

Strange hair colours

Transiting Uranus - Natal Moon

Comfortably out of comfort zone

Freedom from home

Exciting new environment

Disruption to needs

Breaking out of the pattern

Transiting Uranus - Natal Mercury

Bursting with excitement

Interest in all things

Maths, physics, genius, friends, ideas

New ideas, innovations, original thinker

Transiting Uranus - Natal Venus

Independent women become prominent

Autonomous and daring displays of affection

Unusual hobbies and creativity in time with the spirit of the age

Uncommitted, flirtatious, changes in values

Transiting Uranus - Natal Mars

Displays of masculinity with daring

On/off bursts of energy and interest

Urge for excitement

Untamed animal

Unrulable

Transiting Uranus - Natal Jupiter

Insatiable appetite for something different

Traversing further afield

Search, seeking meaning

Trump analysis of philosophy and religion with autonomy

Transiting Uranus - Natal Saturn

Shaking up tradition

Renovating the old unsympathetically

Long term project taking off, or collapsing

Broken bones

Improve efficiency

Transiting Uranus - Natal Uranus

84 years old! (One full cycle of Uranus)

Or mid-life crisis (opposition)

No-one bites you

It's your life

Transiting Uranus - Natal Neptune

A generational movement

Untangling the wooliness

Shaking out the pretence

Transiting Uranus - Natal Pluto

A generational movement

Energy to discard the unnecessary

The wild animal's proof of power

Brilliant transformation

Science enabling changes

Transiting Uranus - Natal North Node

Amazing possibilities

Technological skills

Forward thinking

Spirit of the Age

Transiting Uranus - Natal South Node

Photographs and other digitalized media for posterity

Break from the past

Disruption

Danger of throwing the baby out with the bath water

Transiting Uranus - Ascendant

Piercings, coloured hair, tie-dyed clothes

Festivals and travellers

New-new!-age

Even new-age is old hat

Exciting presentation

Transiting Uranus - Descendant

Other people can be so disruptive

Or exciting

Meeting inspiring people

Challenged to accept other's individuality

Transiting Uranus - M.C

Fit in if you never fit in

Drop out if you were always in

Change of status

Transiting Uranus - I.C

House needs repair

Disruption in the home

Pets

Exciting home life

Move abroad or far away or a very different home life

NEPTUNE transits

♆

NEPTUNE TRANSITS

Neptune transits are so sweet, if you like that insatiable desire for something intangibly divine that can barely be expressed. You end up captivated, day-dreaming, touching the curled edges of a retreating vision. Whether you do or you don't, it makes sense to allow for day-dreaming time.

Listening to music, meditation, inspired dancing and the arts will be a source of relaxation from the desire to find the unfindable.

During this time the world can be perceived as devoid of real beauty and some try to escape. They drink, take drugs, gamble, and tell lies and cheat. Others make the best art they ever made. Religions are sought and sanctuaries are discovered. Shrines are erected. This is a time to make time for the divine.

During Neptune transits the world seems harsh. Water eases the roughness. Swimming and beaches call, with the waves swooshing back and forth, frothing, in constant flux, like your mind.

Stories are invented and poetry sought to ease the soul, by poets who lived tossed by the fascinations, obsessions and desires for the untouchable. Neptune transits connect you, once again, to the sense of oneness in life and to the feeling that there is more to life than just this material world.

Gratitude and compassion can over-flow and bring tears to your eyes. Sometimes, if your eyes are bleary, someone might take advantage of you.

Transiting Neptune - Natal Sun

A mesmerising sense of becoming

Filled with gratitude

Reaching out to help others

Changing jobs, tack or recognizing something creative or divine needs a permanent place in your life

Transiting Neptune - Natal Moon

Need for fluidity

Flowing with family

Divine mothers, men in touch with feelings

Aching for a belonging with true kin

Transiting Neptune - Natal Mercury

Stories and poetry, creative writing

Awareness of speaking inner truth

Mystical texts

Amazing conversations

Elusive, vague and confusing thoughts, speech and situations

Transiting Neptune - Natal Venus

Heightened sense of beauty

Moved within by an aching desire

Longing, limerence, infatuation, fascination

Elusive love, oneness

Day-dreaming and creative imaginings

Transiting Neptune - Natal Mars

Fuzzy boundaries

Sacrificial pursuits

Magnetic and charismatic

Search for divine, some seek alcohol

Swimming/ yoga

Transiting Neptune - Natal Jupiter

Transcendental joy

Kinder world view

Mystical side of religious practices

Relaxed, positive, life affirming

Transiting Neptune - Natal Saturn

Lightening the load, easing ambition

Pleasurable chores and work

Freedom within limitations

A vision sent for manifestation

Transiting Neptune - Natal Uranus

A generational movement

Rounding the edges

Compassion within individuality

Helping less adapted individuals become more autonomous

Transiting Neptune - Natal Neptune

Water, swimming, prayers

Candles, Mystics

Transcendent

Other world

Transiting Neptune - Natal Pluto

A generational movement

Transformation through spiritual practices

Vagueness and confusion around power

Transiting Neptune – Natal North Node

Fascination to reach somewhere

Imagining being better

Searching

Transiting Neptune – Natal South Node

Lost in reincarnations

Vague memories

Nostalgia

Confusion, delusion or modesty over talent

Volunteering and other charitable acts

Transiting Neptune - Ascendant

Being somebody more smooth, mystical, flowing and compassionate

Nautical pursuits, sea, swimming

Artist, poet, story-teller

Counsellor

Transiting Neptune - Descendant

Elusive partner, maybe they drink too much, aren't truthful

Perfect partner, idealized, romantic and fascinating

Woolly boundaries with others

Taken advantage of or equally helped beyond measure

Person with strong Neptune qualities comes into your life

Transiting Neptune – M.C

Recognized as creative, mystical

Work within the Arts or counselling

Ordained

Success with water

Vague values upheld

Retirement

Transiting Neptune I.C

Floods or leaks in the house

Extended family from over-seas

Unsure of lineage

Meditation or holistic practices in the home

Beautiful, calm home environment

Music too

PLUTO

transits

♇

PLUTO TRANSITS

This tiny Planet brings enormous consequences as it transits, back and forth, over a specific degree for years. The intensity and constancy of the universe making a point is unmistakeable. Changes and transformations occur, hopefully through choice. Pluto has a way of wresting old cloaks we treasure from our clinging grasp.

Although all transits bring transformation, the specific realm of Pluto is the id level of our psyche. This is the childish, passionate, unruly and desirous nature which tantrums when it cannot have what it wants. Pluto teaches resilience and foresight. Therefore, the power associated with Pluto is fierce.

Although Pluto represents inner power, there will be many incidences when others abuse their power over you, forcing you to respond. Hopefully, this response would be with inner-strength and not burning resentment seeking revenge, which is also linked to Pluto's realm. If you are abusing your power over others you will not experience the glorious inner strength and more profound meaning.

Pluto in the horoscope is not the underworld of the Greeks; it is deep change through readjustment to power.

Pluto does not bring change like Uranus brings a change of something different. Pluto changes things by its realignment to it. Pluto brings reformation.

The power Pluto awakens is awareness of the 'juice' within the situation or between people.

Transiting Pluto – Natal Sun

Strength, determination to be

Forcing right

Awareness of emotional currents

Transiting Pluto – Natal Moon

Using emotional awareness to effect change

Juicy exchanges

Obsessive and intense

Transiting Pluto - Natal Mercury

Hypnotism, speech altered for effect, manipulation

Throat chakra, occult texts

Intentions set at fundamental level

Clarity, piercing insight

Transiting Pluto – Natal Venus

Attractiveness used for gain

Obsessive, dark and earthy: transformational art

Jealousy and paranoia in close relationships

Damning prophesies from charlatans and other manipulations of your openness.

Transiting Pluto – Natal Mars

Determined, powerful, fear of powerlessness

Anger, force, right and might

Inner strength unsurpassed

Transiting Pluto – Natal Jupiter

Review belief system

Love and fear of God force

Fear of no God

Inner power

God, no God

Transiting Pluto – Natal Saturn

Harsh determination

Adherence to strict limitations

Difficulty letting go

Enforced changes

Transiting Pluto – Natal Uranus

A generational thing

Transformation to destroy old patterns

Including individuals

Transiting Pluto – Natal Neptune

A generational thing

Transforming the notion of spiritual tsunnamis

Engulfing emotional currents

Overcoming the gentle, the addicts or insiduous people

Transiting Pluto – Natal Pluto

Ability to accept change recognized

Watching transformations in slow motion

A generational thing

Justifies

Transiting Pluto – Natal North Node

Re-evaluation of what the future needs

Might not have enough energy to do it oneself

Others may act on your behalf

Transiting Pluto – Natal South Node

Letting go, walking on, moving away

A big pill to swallow

Facing a lifetime of corruption

Transiting Pluto – Natal Ascendant

Accepting power

Not wanting to be small and fearful anymore

Glaring eyes

Inner strength

Ability to seem invisible

Transiting Pluto – Natal Descendant

Danger of assault

Distrusting others

Owning psychological partner

Seeking deeper interactions

Transiting Pluto – Natal M.C

Social pariah or redeemed convict

Fearful, anxious career change

Magnetic authority

Transiting Pluto – Natal I.C

Upsetting changes within family

Sensitized threshold to home

Psychological renovation

Roots

NORTH NODE transits

☊

NORTH NODE TRANSITS

The North Node represents skills and talents which need to be developed for a future life. It is like an unseen support which keeps us moving through time, learning lessons and developing us into meaningful and better people.

The North Node may be difficult to follow. If, in the Natal horoscope, there is no other astrological body conjuncting the North Node, it stands alone and unsupported within a House, opposed by the karmic pull of the South Node.

Focusing on your Natal North Node is a very good practice, as it is said that developing the area of life represented by House and Sign will pull together all the other threads of your life and bind them in one skein.

The North Node has an incredibly positive, yet gentle effect. The North Node awakens the possibilities within the House of the astrological body it transits. Avenues previously not explored may be seen as simple solutions or bridges to a field of interest. This transit brings better ways of doing things as well as integrating new things which are beneficial and meaningful for the future.

Notice how your own Natal North Node brings its teachings, ideas and wisdoms through the transiting North Node.

TRANSITING SOUTH NODE: I have not included the transiting South Node because I do not watch it specifically. When I do, I have found I lose focus and interest in the realm being activated. Though I have noticed (through many charts I have watched) in times of death, shock or misfortune, the South Node has often transited previously, along with a few other transits, over a period of a few days or a week. This has led me to conclude that many, seemingly small, choices and emotional realizations are made for an incident to occur. Where South Node has a link with the concept of Karma, the South Node seems to keep us tied or helps untie knots, according to its inner rule.

Transiting North Node - Natal Sun

Add a new dimension to expressing a natural inclination

Might feel awkward; but worth the effort

Transiting North Node - Natal Moon

Grown up, calm, accepting

Nurturing with a light touch

Attendance to necessities

Transiting North Node - Natal Mercury

Synchronicity of advertising

Emails, words spoken, telephone calls

Apparent normality

Truths spoken, lies made clear

Transiting North Node - Natal Venus

A story unfolds

Emotional reality shared

Meeting people who are good for us

Transiting North Node - Natal Mars

Doing what you know you ought for an interesting, meaningful life

Hauling your body to begin projects

Finding your body wants to do it in another way

Transiting North Node - Natal Jupiter

Freedom to unfold

Openness to new ideas

Future benefits

Transiting North Node - Natal Saturn

Make a commitment and save yourself

Charter a course

Take steps

Transiting North Node - Natal Uranus

Opportunity to do what excites you

But do you dare?

Is your imagination too small?

Will you take the proverbial leap?

Transiting North Node - Natal Neptune

Spiritual environment

Mystical experiences

Air of awakening

Hiding from discontent

Transiting North Node - Natal Pluto

Coolness towards power

Unaffected by mind-games

Light touch to uncover and reveal transformation

Transiting North Node - Natal North Node

How well have you developed this area of your life?

What benefits are there?

What more needs to be done?

What would you be like without these qualities?

Transiting North Node - Natal South Node

Integrating new behaviours with old behaviours

Making habitual patterns more palatable

Creating space in the mind

Pauses before triggers and unthinking expressions

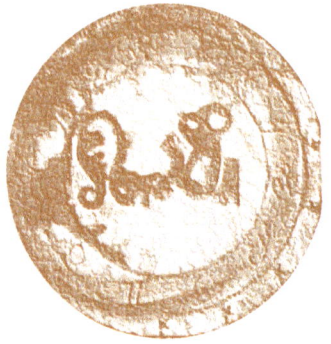

Transiting North Node - Ascendant

Watching how others do it and copying

Trying to act smoothly

Being smooth and careful

Seamless, natural, easy

Transiting North Node - Descendant

Other people who are good for you

Keeping in touch or saying goodbye is not the issue

Sharing what is real at that time

Transiting North Node - M.C

Seen as an individual in your own right, with all your facets and accepting all your roles, you take each part responsibly.

Transiting North Node - I.C

Returning home

Beginning a new way

Letting go of the old

Practicing in private

Using home productively

DATE	TRANSIT

DATE	TRANSIT

DATE	TRANSIT

NOTES: **notes about notes: new concepts, new ideas to check out later: draw the symbols and make them my own: the symbol which fascinates me most right now is....fascinations change as I develop: notes about other people who bring out a Planetary energy in me: notes:**

Also published by Fishtail Arts & Astrology:

Manual of Astrological Calculations 2019

Just Cosmic 2018

Cosmic Journal 2018

Age of the Fishtail 2013

www.fishtailarts.com

www.cosmicjournal.co.uk

FB Fishtail Arts & Astrology

Astro Journal by Rikki Blythe

Published by Fishtail Arts & Astrology

 2018